Genevieve Whitford

The Sound of The Harp

by

Genevieve Smith Whitford

Genevieve Smith Whitford
is the author of

QUEEN ANNE'S LACE

Harp Press   1982
Harp Press   1983
Macmillan Publishers   1987
Harp Press   1990

THE SOUND OF THE HARP

Harp Press   1989
Harp Press   1991

Art direction and illustrations
by
Sara Donovan Whitford

Copyright 1989
ISBN 0-9610456-1-2

HARP PRESS
201 West Evergreen Avenue Suite 904
Philadelphia, Pennsylvania 19118
(215) 248-9860

To the poet, all things are friendly and sacred, all events profitable, all days holy, all men divine.

Emerson

For George, with my love.

The Sound of the Harp

Though I have played the harp for most of my life, I am not a musician. I was interested more in ideas than in music, and had neither the aptitude nor the energy to master an instrument. But a harp is not easily left behind, so it went with me to Philadelphia when we married and then back and forth across the country as we moved. Through the busy years of householding and child rearing, the harp was often unstrung, and so was I. But sometimes, when the children were in bed, I practiced, and all of my children have happy memories of going to sleep to the sound of the harp. I didn't know they were listening.

Genevieve Whitford

In ancient Greece, the word *himeros* was used to describe poetry and the harp, and it meant *beauty that makes the heart yearn.*

Of Poetry and Harps

What do the words of the poet
have to do
with the sound of the harp?
Both play on the taut strings
of our gut emotions.
Both find harmony
in the chaos of our lives.
Both touch that throbbing center
of ourselves
that beats in concert
with all humankind.

First Love

We were cousins,
played together
when we were only three.
He was all boy,
sturdy,
square compared to me.
I remember cotton rompers
and a pock-marked doll
named Liz,
summer days of make-believe,
when he was father,
I, the mother,
until it palled,
and then we changed around
for him to mind the dolls
while I took off
on tricycle
to see the world.
He was strong
and gentle
and fair.
I look for him
in all men,
and find him
in the men
I love.

The New Baby

I remember
standing in the doorway
sobbing
because Mother was hurting
and Daddy was taking her
to the hospital.
I could see her
waiting in the car
at the end of the walk
as he turned to give me
one last kiss.
There was excitement
in the air,
and promise,
but I felt only grief
and loss.

Baby Brother

You were beautiful to me,
as neither my own children
nor my grandchildren would be.
With what pride I showed you off,
stark naked,
to the passersby on Longwood Drive,
and how they smiled to see
a Cupid with his arrows spent
on a girl child smitten
with first stirrings
of maternity.

The First Day of School

It was cold outside,
and the cloakroom smelled of wet boots
as I huddled there
on the first day of school,
afraid to brave the larger room,
with its rigid rows
of sturdy desks,
each one like the other.
How was I to find my place
in this new world
of strangers?

What Is Marriage?

Marriage is
trust in each other,
faith in the future,
commitment to life.
Marriage means
that I love you
for what you are,
and I will honor you
for what you become.
In marriage
we create life
as we were created,
we nurture life
as we were nurtured,
we promise life
for generations to come.
In marriage we say,
Yes!
I do!
I will!
to *life*.

Holy Men

Let them read from dead scrolls
or bow before priests
or take to the woods
with their gurus.
I will learn more
of loving and living
and life after death
from the baby I hold
in my arms.

The Woman Astronaut

"It was incredible!"
said the astronaut
of her first flight
into space.
But sometime she'll know
that nothing compares
with the awesome experience
of giving birth
to a baby.

Mother and Child

When a woman stands
with a child in her arms,
she sways
with the rhythm
of the universe.

Balloons

How many bright balloons
have slipped away from me,
by accident
or carelessness,
out of hand
and out of reach,
inflated dreams,
so transient,
yet beautiful to see
as they drift aimlessly
into obscurity.

Corporate Wife's Response

Why do I swear at a door knob?
Because door knobs lose their screws.
Why do I scream at an innocent child?
Because children lose their shoes.
Why do I cry over sugar?
It spills on the floor and grows there.
Why do I curse the dog?
He knows the best rug and he goes there.
Clocks always need winding,
toasters break down,
sox lose their mates,
bananas turn brown,
laundry piles up,
bills go unpaid,
and if I don't make them,
the beds are unmade.
So why am I taking it out on you?
Because you have a secretary
and a maintenance crew.

To a Child Stillborn

I never held you in my arms
nor suckled you
but oh, how close we were,
those many months
when you were cradled
in my womb.
With my own blood
I nourished you
and would have given life
for you to live
but you could not survive
apart from me.
Now in your place
another child bestirs
who never would have been conceived
if you had lived,
your gift to us of life
by sacrifice,
that we might learn
to live again
for that which is,
and not what might have been.

When You Were Seventeen

When you were seventeen
you took me in your arms and said
"I've given you a bad time,
haven't I, Mother?"
and we both cried.
A bad time?
Does it matter
that you lived in ragged T-shirts
and that your room was a disaster
compounded by dirty clothes
and barbells
and unfinished assignments?
Wasn't it natural
to argue over when to be home
and to put aside your books
to sing and dance your way
through ANNIE GET YOUR GUN?
You were always a good student
and a good citizen.
Everyone admired you
and we were very proud of you.
In your last year at home
you behaved normally
for a teen-ager
and we reacted normally
as parents.

Much as we loved you
we knew that it was time
to let you go.
You were ready
and so were we.
But thank you for the hug
and the cleansing tears.

My House Through Mary's Eyes

My house is filled with sunshine now,
and polished wood
and photographs
of smiling children.
Mary doesn't know
the dark days
we lived through.
The ambience she envies
is of ordinary things,
alternately scarred
by life's abrasions
and restored
by sweat and tears.

A Woman's Scorn

You say you do not love me anymore.
What do you mean by love?
That I no longer have the power
to titilate?
I can't compete with her firm flesh,
for mine is stretched from pregnancy.
Is it variety you need?
Where is excitement greater
than the sum of all our joys
and sorrows?
Is her affection worth more
than the love of children
you betrayed?
I should not grieve.
I have lost only my illusions.
You have lost your place,
become an aberration
in the chain of generations.

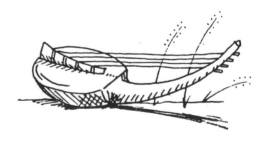

Woman Talk

Maggie does day work for a living
and I am the lady of the house
but when she comes to clean
we visit like old friends.
She left school at fifteen,
married at sixteen,
and had five children
by the time she was twenty-three.
She is young enough
to be my daughter,
but our differences are less
than the things we have
in common.
We have both given birth
and faced the death of loved ones.
We have coped with parents,
husbands and children,
and now we worry over our grandchildren.
Our joys and sorrows are the same
and it helps to share them.

Maggie

Maggie grew up on a farm
and didn't know she was poor,
but her sister remembers
the shame she felt
when she had to take thick slices
of Ma's homemade bread
in her school lunch
because they couldn't afford
store bread.

Maggie Remembers

"Someone from the welfare office
brought presents for our Christmas . . .
a cradle for me,
but I didn't have a doll
so I wrapped a log
in a piece of cloth
and rocked it to sleep."

Maggie's Aunts

"My aunts never liked my mother.
They thought Pa married
beneath himself.
But he drank so much that sometimes
there was no money for us.
When we needed shoes
or had to see a dentist,
Ma would send us over the hill
to our aunts' house.
They kept pretty dresses there
for our trips into town,
but we could never wear them
home."

Maggie Said

"I couldn't cry when my father died.
I wanted to beat him with my fists
for all the hurt he'd done
to Ma and to us . . .
but I didn't.
What would the undertaker think
if he came in black and blue?
Do dead men bruise?"

The Curse

"I keep dreaming about my father.
He comes asking about his car
and gives us hell
for moving into his house.
I scream at him, 'Go away!
You're dead! Go away!'
but he stays there,
cursing."

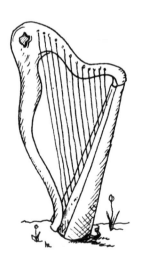

Nature's Way

The baby kangaroo
slips from the womb,
a half-formed fetus,
but he knows
the way to go
to find his mother's pouch,
and it is up,
and so he struggles
against gravity
to the warmth and food
that will sustain him.
Whence comes his certainty,
and how did we lose ours?
How can we question
in our lives
the wisdom
of that inborn sense
that guides birds
across continents,
sends salmon up the stream
to spawn,
leads baby turtles
to the safety of the sea,
and accounts for the billions
of life forms
that have developed
and survived
without man's intervention.

To Be A Man

To be a man and not a beast
is inhibiting,
even in primitive societies,
where every man's passion
must be controlled
for the good of the group.
We inherit the yoke of civilization
from our fathers,
and would lose our way without it,
but we stumble under the weight of it
and our instincts atrophy.
We need a sexologist
to tell us how to mate,
and a psychiatrist
to interpret our dreams.
We need a doctor
to deliver our babies
and a formula to feed them.
We go to gymnasiums
to learn how to exercise,
to conservatories
to learn how to sing,
and to universities
to learn how to think.
Animals must know
that we have taken leave of our senses
as they run from us to the safety
of their burrows and their caves.

Healing

She lies there mangled
and I cannot pray for her
for I know no god
who listens
to my prayers.
Nor can my willing her to live
suffice,
my will is such a small,
weak thing.
But I have faith
that's strong and reassuring,
that hemorrhaging will stop,
that bones will mend,
and when the swelling goes,
her mind will clear
and sight will be restored.
The drive in nature is to heal,
to grow,
regenerate.
This is the power
that gives us hope,
that doctors emulate.

The Encyclopedia and the Crèche

It's time again to move the encyclopedia,
all twenty-four volumes
plus the index and the atlas,
to make room for the crèche.
Not that we believe
in the myth of the virgin birth,
but it's a lovely story about a baby,
the son of God,
born to bring peace to a warring world.
We are all the children of God,
born to love and be loved.
Through each other, we honor Him.
We gather on His birthday
to restore ourselves with elemental things:
to warm ourselves by the fire,
to light our way with candles,
to nourish ourselves
with shared food and drink.
We marvel at the tree,
whose every bauble is a memory,
and we give and receive gifts
which are wrapped in love, however clumsily.
In the holidays, we celebrate
life and love and hope
with a faith too easily put aside
to make room for the definitions and analysis
of the encyclopedia
which describe the world in great detail
but lack the power to save it.

The Diver

He is no one to me,
that strange young man,
yet when he dives
in cresting wave
and disappears
into the sea,
I hold my breath,
for he is every child
I ever loved
who rode the waves
to test himself
and me.

Once a Mother

When a baby cries,
my breasts still fill with milk,
or so it seems,
though I am much too old.
When a child is hurt,
I want to hold her close,
whomever she may be.
I drive carefully around the cyclist,
in whose slight frame
and vulnerability,
I see my sons,
and I am not at all surprised
to find that he is black.

Let It Be

Will you not let it be,
small man?
The drifted snow,
the patterned fields,
the mountain peaks
exist without your comment.
You talk too much.
Your conversation
wafts across the aisle
and over seats.
Steward, bring his tray.
Silence him with food.
He interrupts our reverie,
intrudes himself
on natural wonders
we would like to see.

Mrs. Armentrout

She was the grande dame
of the nursing home.
She moved in with her pearls
and her carved teakwood chairs
and her sterling silver brush and comb,
and she kept white kid gloves
in a satin box
in the top drawer
of her dresser.
When you stopped by her door,
she invited you in for tea,
which you politely refused
because you knew
that the porcelain pot was empty
and the cups long since gone
with the rest of her goods.
Suddenly she sickened
and took to her bed
and finally died,
and I always felt
it had to do
with the plastic roses
that came from a well-meaning friend
who didn't know
that some of us are violently allergic
to plastic.

On the Subway

The old woman shifts her burden
and reaches for the strap
to keep from falling
on the young man dozing comfortably
under a sign that reads,
"These seats reserved for the aged and infirm."

The wino talks to himself,
(who else will listen?)
sometimes mumbling,
sometimes crying out obscenities.

The woman with the brief case frowns,
anticipating chaos at home
after the order of indexed files
in the steel cabinets of her office.

The violinist braces his instrument
between his knees,
his emotions locked in its frayed case.

The man in the gray flannel suit
hides behind the *Wall Street Journal*,
hoping to find himself in the statistics,
or on a graph, moving up.

A frazzled woman spreads her legs
to make a lap for the Bloomingdale bag
overflowing with packaged amenities.

The young girls giggle irrepressibly,
forgetting that laughter
is a public nuisance.

The school boys punch each other,
too young to know that we must learn
to live together without touching.

The waiter sits self-consciously
in his worn tuxedo,
wondering why no one will publish
his Great American Novel.

The child sits on his mother's lap,
solaced by his thumb,
silenced by the empty looks
of those who would deny his existence.

The rest of us stare blankly at each other,
not wanting to intrude,
afraid to see, reflected,
our anonymity.

My Grandmother

I remember
silver plate
wreathed in rosebuds,
and Blue Willow dishes
on her table,
and pieces of wedding cake
turning to dust
in a glass jar
in her cupboard,
and bleeding hearts
in her garden
that seemed to cry with her
over the dreams
that died in her
in the remorseless heat
of the prairie.

As a Bride

You chose bright plastic
plates and mugs
from Denmark
for your table,
and by the time you asked
for Grandmother's Blue Willow dishes,
they were gone.

Cherubim

When you were a baby
I wanted a picture of myself
holding you,
witness to the miracle
of birth.
But time was short
and portraits dear,
and you grew out of my arms.
Then I wanted to carve
a likeness of you,
to fix your round cheeks,
your turned up nose,
your rosebud mouth,
in marble.
But I was not a Michelangelo,
and no one less would do.
Now I know
that it was childhood
I would capture
if I could,
and motherhood.
Artists through the ages
have sculpted you.
In museums everywhere,
I find you
among the cherubs,
and myself
in the madonnas.

On Observing Grandchildren

Girls are flowers,
unfolding,
fecund,
meant by nature
to blossom,
to bear fruit,
and to drop their seed.
What noble purpose,
to give beauty,
to nourish
and replenish life.

Boys are flexing muscle,
animal,
strong,
protective,
daring to explore
and change
the world.

To a Grandchild

Thank you for looking like your mother,
for giving us a hand to hold
and a child to hug,
when we thought she'd grown
away from us.
You are our seed,
and your blossoming keeps us growing
into the future.

Thank you for being your own person,
and for bringing your father's genes
into our family
to enrich us with new strengths
and possibilities.

Thank you for your laughter,
which is contagious,
and for your tears,
which show us that you care.
Is it any wonder that we love you?

The Suicide

She looked through eyes that magnified
until the light blinded her
and she stumbled into darkness.

She listened so intently
that words echoed in her mind
and became a deafening roar.

She felt so deeply
that even love became a burden
too heavy to bear.

Dear one, rest in peace.

Dilemma

If I could be
what I try to be
when I'm with you,
then I'd be true
to no one.

Muffled Cries

In the early morning hours
of a gray October day,
I waken to the muffled cries
of birds, I think, migrating south,
away from winter's cold.
And then I know,
from knowledge born of fear,
that these sounds come,
not from the skies,
but from my father's room
across the hall,
the wheezing
of his mucous-laden breath
as he lies struggling
against the winter
of his ninetieth year.

Pictures on the Wall

There stands my father,
younger than my son,
and he, the baby
in another frame,
is father now,
and I, who walk
the corridor between,
hold them both in close embrace,
and they are one.

Every Woman Knows

There is no room for Mother
when you move into his heart.
She is gently relegated
to his mind,
encased in gratitude,
but kept apart emotionally
from fear of falling
into old dependencies.
And she is happy there.
As a man, her son is strength
and joy,
but she can live without him.
It is the child he was
that she carries in her heart,
and would not share with any woman,
even with his wife.

Mother Love

I give you love
but do not ask it back
lest it should die with me.
It is for you to give
to spouse, to children
and to friends,
that I may see it grow
and know
that it flows endlessly
from me.

To a Son

I loved you as a baby
and I loved you as a boy,
but to know you as a man
is a special kind of joy.

Marriage

I've been thinking about marriage lately,
not about our own because
George and I have been together
for so long
that he seems a part of me,
and I don't fuss over any part of myself
unless it's hurting.
We feel good about ourselves
and each other
and I don't know what I'd do
without him.
We agree with the same editorials
and laugh at the same jokes
and like the same people
and hold hands watching television,
which somehow gives us hope
for the future
in spite of the news.
What worries me are the divorce statistics,
the number of couples
who don't stay together long enough
to rediscover each other
after the trying years
of raising children
are over.

I worry about the Lockhorns
and the cartoons in the *New Yorker*
of nagging wives
and grouchy husbands
in tragi-comic confrontation.
More depressing are the pictures
in small town newspapers
of Golden Anniversary couples,
those marcelled women
and tired looking men
who will stand together
in some church basement
to be congratulated on surviving.
She has long since lost her sex appeal
and settled for pats on the fanny
in the kitchen,
and he looks more interested
in cost accounting
or the back forty
than in romance.
Still, I am haunted
by the distraught old man I saw
in the corridor of the hospital
where his wife had just died.
He was leaning against the wall,
comforted by a son and a daughter,
and he said, "Please don't leave me,
I can't go home alone."

Love and Marriage

When we were young
he brought me flowers
for the prom,
small be-ribboned clusters
of sweetheart roses
and baby's breath
that wilted on my breast
in the heat of the dance,
and we called it love.

Now, each Saturday,
he comes from the Farmer's Market
with tall spears
of flaming gladioli,
and crusty homemade bread
and white and yellow cheeses
and shiney purple eggplants
and ruffled green lettuce
and plump red tomatoes
and Hickory nuts
and raspberries,
even in October,
and we call it marriage.

Why Marry?

They say that it is better far
to marry than to burn,
but in today's society
there is no cause to yearn,
for a casual relationship
can end with you in bed
without the complication
of ever being wed.

Marriage is

caring, sharing, bearing;
holding, folding, molding;
keeping, sweeping, weeping;
earning, yearning, burning;
assurance, insurance, endurance.

Erotica

In my erotic dreams
I am a whore,
waiting
behind an unfamiliar door,
my firm young body
loosely wrapped
in satin
which will fall away
in time
and leave me naked.

I have kept my marriage vows
and spent my days
in wifery.
I have borne children,
raised them well,
and lived to know their young.
But underneath the apron
of my propriety
a part of me remains
uncalloused,
clothed in gossamer
and free.

Reflection III

We grow closer with the years,
my aging self and aging brother.
I lean on him as I see in him
the shadow of our father,
and he clings to me
as he sees in me,
reflections of our mother.

The Death of a Brother

Your children knew
the grief you felt
when your brother died,
for they could see
that rivalry
must sometime end,
lest one should die
before the healing words
of love
are spoken.

Generation

Your genes are from
a great grandfather
on my mother's side
who was the youngest son
of a youngest son,
without property,
who migrated from Germany
to homestead in Nebraska.
Your genes are from his son,
who grew up in a sod house,
who had little schooling
but loved to read,
who minded the baby
while his mother worked
in the fields,
and who saw their crops destroyed
by black clouds of grasshoppers.
Your genes are from his wife,
my grandmother,
a school teacher,
who never forgave him
for the hardships she endured
on the prairie,
and who told her daughter,
who told me,
that he sucked the milk
from her breast
when the pain of an abcess
was unbearable,
and there was no doctor
to lance it.

Your genes are from
a great grandfather
on my father's side,
who moved to Michigan
to homestead
when his factory burned
in Connecticut,
and who brought some of New England
with him:
a rosewood piano,
a respect for learning,
and a dedication
to the Congregational Church
which he built in the wilderness,
and which still marries and buries and blesses
his descendants.
Your genes are from his son,
who became a gentleman farmer,
who bred fine cattle
and ran for governor
and sent his children to boarding school,
though he never had any money.
And the grandmother,
who lived by the Lord
and succored the poor
and wrote her children
to lead a Christian life
when they were away from home.
Your genes are from
their intelligent, dispassionate son,
my father,

who was a scientist
but who loved the opera
and sang tenor,
which harmony echoes
in every song I hear.
Your genes are from
the beautiful girl he married,
who was his secretary
and my mother,
daughter of the pioneer,
who wanted to go to college
but couldn't,
who scorned women's work
but loved her family,
who was active in the community
and designed houses,
but was ever ruled by her heart
and her prejudices
which both warmed and enraged me.
Your genes include those from your father,
whose great grandfather
was Canadian,
Counselor to the Queen,
whose son was a doctor,
who moved to Colorado
with his consumptive wife
who bore him four children
and outlived him.
And the other grandfather
with the improbable name
of Carlos Pedro

attached to the surname
of Whitford,
who worked in insurance
and was mayor of Beloit.
And his son, your grandfather,
a quiet man
who married the doctor's daughter,
a vivacious girl
who loved people
and mothering
and cooking
and who raised two sons.
Your father was the eldest,
a serious fellow
who became a big man on campus,
and then a big man in insurance,
who enjoyed his work
and loved his family
and played a mean piano.
Your genes are from your mother,
who wanted to write
and change the world,
who loved her family,
but rebelled against women's work,
who sometimes played the harp
and now writes poetry.

These are your genes,
refined in prosperity,
strengthened by adversity.
Use them well!

Legacies

From my mother,
open arms,
from my father,
an open mind,
from my husband,
an open hand,
and from my children,
an open heart,
for in their need,
they taught me to love.

There is No Middle Age

There is no middle age.
You're either old or you are young.
You say, "Yes, sir!" for half your life,
while climbing, rung by rung,
up the ladder of success,
but when you reach the top,
you're done!

You're the young one on committees,
half afraid to speak your mind,
then you're chairman ex-officio,
with duties left behind.

You're the newest of vice-presidents,
with a carpet on the floor,
but before you've done your job,
another name is on your door.

You learn to raise your children
by the time they've gone from home.
When you have the time and money,
you no longer care to roam.

You're too liberal for your father
and too stodgy for your son.
You've debated all the issues
but you feel you've never won.

You spend a lifetime learning.
Do you then become a sage?
You never know how little you know
till you're well past middle age.

The Eye of the Beholder

"You are beautiful" he says,
and I search the mirror to see
what it is that he still finds
beautiful in me.
Moonlight
from a long-remembered shore,
good-byes
from a long forgotten war,
mysteries,
long ago revealed,
promises,
in rapture sealed,
now fulfilled.

Delayed Reaction

Why do I see myself
in the girl on the bicycle
or the student in the classroom
or the model in the magazine
or the young mother with her children,
but never in the aging woman
who stares at me so insistently
from every mirror that I pass?

CAT Scan

I lie motionless on the metal cart
that glides slowly, majestically,
into the awesome other-world
of the cathode machine.
I breath and stop breathing
in response to the muffled voice
of an attendant carefully shielded
from the rays that bombard me.
They penetrate my body
to uncover my darkest secrets,
lesions that could destroy me.
I am quiet, hoping to escape the truth.

In the room across the hall,
a young couple waits
for word from the doctor.
"It is twins!" he says.
The young woman catches her breath
then laughs.
She cannot stop laughing
and her happiness flows down the corridor,
touching everyone.
I think of the changes in their life,
and in ours,
but I cannot grieve.
Their joy is contagious
and I laugh with them.

The Hospital

The door opens without my touch,
and closes automatically
against the world.
I am assigned to a cubicle
by computer,
stripped of my identity
along with my clothes,
and reduced to a set of statistics
on a chart.
My will is taken away,
with my money and my rings,
for my own protection.
My pride is stored in a plastic cup
with my removable bridge.
My mind and my heart
become less interesting
than blood and urine.
Within hours, I will be drugged
and assaulted
by masked strangers with knives
who will determine my future
while I sleep.
Ye god-like monitors
of my heartbeat and my aspiration,
don't mistake me for the bloody sheets
you change routinely
and throw aside so carelessly
to be sanitized and bleached!

The Druggist Likes Me As I Am

My blood is laced with cortisone,
my heart is fibrillating,
my bones are losing calcium,
my muscles, stiff and aching.
My teeth are full of cavities,
my stomach's gone to pot,
my heartburn interferes with sleep,
my energy is shot.
My hair is getting grayer,
my eyes are growing dim;
if I don't control my moustache
I'll be taken for a him.
With all the subterfuge required,
the costly reconstruction,
is there anything about me
that is safe from this destruction?
The running down, the wearing out
is there for all to see
and I have to fight it daily,
but it isn't really me.
That's in my poetry.

If I Were Young Again

If I were young again
I'd wear white dimity
and lace
and flowers in my hair.
I'd swim naked in the moonlight
and make love on mossy rocks
beside the sea.
I'd sing and dance
and try to capture
on my canvas
sun refracted from the leaves
of trees.

I was old when I was young,
trying to probe the mysteries
of life and death.
Now I know that they endure
without my knowledge
or consent.
Death is unseen, unfelt,
of passing interest
to him who carves our name
and final date
on stone.
Life is our response,
to sights and sounds,
to words of truth,
to acts of love.
All else is postscript,
even poetry.

When I Die

When I die,
don't put a stone on me
and leave me to rot
with strangers.
Take me to the village
where my father was born,
to the church yard
where he and my mother
lie buried,
and where all the tombstones
are of family
and friends.
Scatter my ashes
on our common ground
and plant a tree nearby,
that I may nourish roots
and keep on growing.

On Being Published

A part of me
is out there now,
exposed
and irretrievable,
to be ignored
or brought to life
by spark of recognition
in the hearts and minds
of others.